KW-573-464

Published poems by the author

'Landlord of All': *Poetry Now Northern England 2000*, Poetry Now. ISBN 0754308022.

'Soldiers of Christ': *Prominent Voices*, Poetry Now. ISBN 0754308723.

'Soldiers of Christ': *Christian Verse from the UK,* Triumph Herald. ISBN 1861612885.

'From Acorn to Oak': *Poems of Faith*, Triumph Herald. ISBN 1861611420.

'Strength in Our Need': *A True Companion*, Triumph Herald. ISBN 1861611315.

'What is Love?': *Light of the Soul*, Triumph Herald. ISBN 1861611226.

'The Lost Youth of Merrie England': *Spring Bards*, Arrival Press. ISBN 1857865758.

'The Symbol of Slaughtered Youth': *Fallen Heroes*, Arrival Press. ISBN 1857865855.

'Remembrance of Emily': *Seeing and Feeling*, Women's Words. ISBN 0754304590.

'The Challenge of Peace': *The Poetic 100-year Diary*, Poetry Now. ISBN 1861884710.

'Hidden by Time': *Poetry Now North West 1997*, Poetry Now. ISBN 1861884737.

'The Tearful Years': *For the Children*, Triumph Herald. ISBN 1861610777.

'The Passage of Time': *Growing with God*, Triumph Herald. ISBN 1861610084.

'Days of Yore': *The Good Ol' Days*, Arrival Press. ISBN 1857864794.

'Time is Running Out': *Hopes for the Future*, Poetry Now. ISBN 1861884400.

'Journey of the Mind': *Destinations*, Poetry Now. ISBN 1861884230.

'Forgotten Meaning': *A Christian Gift*, Triumph Herald. 1861610742.

'Forgotten Meaning': *The Rhythm of Life*, Triumph Herald. ISBN 1861611722.

'Faded Memories': *New Rhymes for the Children*, Arrival Press. ISBN 1857865162.

'Judgement's Clock': *At the Third Stroke*, Poetry Now. ISBN 185731672X

'Ladies of the Night': *Fallen Angels*, Poetry Now. ISBN 1857316339.

'To Angel, my friend': *Poetic Letters*, Poetry Now. ISBN 1861664117.

'The Future Foretold': *A Paler Shade of Green*, Poetry Now. ISBN 1861884915.

'Man's Destiny Foretold': *Our Hopes for the Future,* Triumph Herald. ISBN 1861610440.

'Countdown to Change': *A Chance for Charity*, Triumph Herald. ISBN 1861611005.

'Pandora's Box': *Spreading the Word*, Triumph Herald. ISBN 1861611218.

'Hidden World': *Street Life*, Poetry Now. ISBN 1861885903.

'Broken Union': *Larger Than Life*, Arrival Press. ISBN 1857865863.

'In Memorial': *Along the Way*, Triumph Herald. ISBN 1861614357.

'Let love blossom in your heart for all': *The Love we call our own*, Poetry Now. ISBN 0754308944.

'God's Loving Embrace': *Garden of Peace,* Triumph Herald. ISBN 1861611013.

'Pleas From the Heart': *Peotry Now North West Anthology*, Peotry Now. ISBN 1857316223.

All the above publishers are part of the same group:
Forward Press Ltd. Remus House, Coltsfoot Drive, Woodston, Peterborough, PE2 9JX.
www.forwardpress.co.uk

Poetry Library
104396
COPY NO. 2

Images from Within

WITHDRAWN FROM THE POETRY LIBRARY

Sculpture in the Garden: Cover Motif

The cover motif is based on a sculpture by Stephen Broadbent in the Cloister Garden of Chester Cathedral.

The sculpture is inspired by the story of Jesus and the Woman of Samaria in John 4. He asked her for a drink of water, and in return she received the water of eternal life. The Woman's faith and life are seen here to stem directly from Jesus himself

The Very Reverend Dr Stephen S Smalley
Dean of Chester Cathedral

Images from Within

Poems and Prose

Jane Dyson

Writers Club Press
San Jose New York Lincoln Shanghai

Images from Within
Poems and Prose

All Rights Reserved © 2000 by Jane Dyson

No part of this book may be reproduced or transmitted in any form or by any means, graphic, electronic, or mechanical, including photocopying, recording, taping, or by any information storage or retrieval system, without the permission in writing from the publisher.

Published by Writers Club Press
an imprint of iUniverse.com, Inc.

For information address:
iUniverse.com, Inc.
620 North 48th Street
Suite 201
Lincoln, NE 68504-3467
www.iuniverse.com

ISBN: 0-595-00569-1

Printed in the United States of America

To the Dean and Chapter of Chester Cathedral, without whose aid I would never have come to faith.

Contents

Foreword

Touching evocative imagery makes these poetic word pictures appealing to all. Visualise the places captured, the feelings evoked, and let the poet hold your attention provoking unexpected responses.

These beguiling poems, sometimes deceptively simple and easy to read, embody deep thoughts. The genuine feeling they express is that of a committed Christian who has confronted the world we all live in – with sincerity, understanding love and resolved conflict or pain. Some of the poems I found especially moving: *Pleas from the Heart, To Angel My Friend, In Memorial:* in these the poet's insight into personal conflict and pain is expressed poignantly, with a simplicity and directness that conveys the depths of thought and feeling with immediate impact.

As one reads these gems of love and understanding, one cannot but help feel the poet's muse is not a mythical, winged Pegasus that surveys the world from above, detached and philosophical, but a guardian angel, a close companion who lovingly opens her eyes to the simple but real things of our everyday life. From the heart-searching imagery of World War I to playtime on a rainy day for children jumping into puddles as the rain falls down – all hit chords whatever one's age. Let the words lighten your darkness.

Charles Muller

MA (Wales) PhD (Lond) DLitt (OFS) DEd (SA)

I

Poems

The Landlord of All

In these days of wealth and material things
We seem to have forgotten the one that made all that life brings.
We lounge around, doing what we feel,
We take what we want without any thought
About who it is hurting, who can do nought.

For our modern life has only one creed:
We covet the things others possess,
We heed not the pain, nor the distress
That's engendered through man's insatiable greed
When our light-fingered touch encounters our need.
Yet is it a need, or really a vice? It's certainly a sin, this avarice!

This constant collecting of things not our own!
Why not pick up the phone, or return all to their proper home?
Nothing on Earth is truly one's own.
We are but tenants of the Landlord of all,
And all will be redeemed at his Trumpet call!

Bare your soul while there's still time,
Be it a sixpence, half pence or a dime!
Whatever the sum, it's still a crime.
Reduce the cost of your hidden sin,
For who knows when the Landlord will come in!

Soldiers of Christ

Do not mourn for things that cannot be!
Turn your thoughts to Christ's sacrifice on Calvary;
As Christ did, do the same,
Shoulder your cross, march bravely on,
We are all soldiers in Christ.

Our backs may be bowed with the pressures we face,
But we march, knowing we're wrapped in God's grace.
Follow his footsteps: wherever he leads, follow,
Be not one to wallow in grief!
Talk to your Saviour! Gain your relief!

Turn to face each new day,
Bend your knees and pray.
Be not ashamed; pick up your cross,
Follow your Saviour—he'll show you the way
For we are all soldiers in Christ!

God's Loving Embrace

Pauvre petit my little *fleurs*,
Raising their heads, to feel the sun
Tenderly caressing their innocent faces,
Welcoming God's loving embrace.

Their undaunted trust shows
What we humans forget,
That God's omniscient power is always around,
Cushioning us from Satanic temptation.

The *fleurs* in the garden show us the way,
That faith in his holiness can never be lost,
No matter what sorrow, vexation and cost.
He'll always be, within our reach.

Cast away your sorrows,
Make God your friend
Pauvre petit fleurs
Will win in the end.

Have Trust in the Lord

There it stands, silhouetted on the crest of the hill,
The cross that ended Jesus' ministry.
With sun gleaming on the crown of thorns
That adorn that humble head
Bowed down with the sins of man.

Man forgets too readily what Jesus did for him,
Absolving him from every sin.
Cast off thy fetters of mortal life,
Place your trust in everlasting life.

Accept God's bounty, loudly proclaim:
Bow not your head in shame!
Walk boldly on, calmly
Place your trust in the Lord.

The Colourful Seasons

Green is the herald of Spring
With dew soaked grass, bursting buds,
Ferns and flowering plants,
And many dainty things!

Yellow is the heat of the Summer sun,
Tempting naked bodies to bask beneath its burning rays!
Golden heads wave in the gentle breeze
That caresses the heated skin.

Brown is the Lord of Autumn's array,
Leaves falling, a many-coloured hue:
Branches bare, furrows deep
As nature prepares the earth for sleep.

Winter with its white chilly coat is here,
Ice and snow adorning nature's icy veil:
She hides the resting, weary earth
Beneath this mantle white.

There it stays, safe and warm
Till Spring pokes out its green coat tails:
Once more the cycle awakens, from sleep
To early morning dews.

From Acorn to Oak

From acorn to oak we watch them grow,
Never knowing when sorrows will show!
The same is true of our daily life:
The canker of depression must be lanced with a knife.

Forget your pains, your fears, your toil!
Like the tiny acorn, planted in fertile soil,
Welcome the rise, of each newborn day,
Whimper not, but go out to play.

Make the most of every hour,
Revel in the sunlight like the fresh-blooming flower;
All it takes is a determined stance
And a wish to give this world a second chance.

Then one day you'll open your eyes and say
'Good Morning' to the brand new day!
Your heart's lighter, you feel so gay!
Don't just read this and put the book away!

When trials come, as come they must,
Outface your sorrows and seek your rest.
Put your trust in God—He'll do the rest!
Be sure to put this good advice to the test.

Strength in Our Need

Stop and think, who gave us life
At the dawn of creation,
When all things were right.
Remember this when there comes a day
When the blues will out and you give way:
God is your ever faithful, caring friend,
He'll be with you till the end.
Never doubt this is true!
He'll comfort you and see you through.
You just need to stop and pray.
Even though he's with us every day,
It's only right we should ask
That he turn his great heart to our humble task.
Remember, though friends may come and go,
God's here for all of us, you know.

What is Love?

Who truly knows, what love is?
For each, it means something uniquely different,
Whether it be the love of a mother for her child,
Or the love between a husband and wife,
Pitted as it often is with troubles and strife.
Or the love between two people, of the same gender and sex;
Should we abuse them for what they cannot help?
After all, we're all God's creatures,
And His heart is big enough for all.
He loves each and every one of us
Despite what human emotions we feel.
He does not colour his love this way:
To him, love is the ideal!
His own teaching tells us
To love thy neighbour as thy self,
So what gives man the right
To make distinctions 'about something we cannot help'?
Each to his own is what love should really be!
We should dwell in God's sweet love
And reside in true harmony.

Jane Dyson

The Lost Youth of Merrie England

By their thousands they went,
Men, young brawny and strong,
Travelled through the shrouded night
Across the moonlit seas
To the land where destiny awaits,
Some, never to return,
To Merrie England's Island Fortress,
Home to you and me.

They went away, both young and strong,
And those that did return,
Having passed through the devil's cauldron,
Of futility and despair,
The ramparts may have faltered,
But never did they fall,
The Youth of Merrie England,
Who answered her country's call.

Some dreamed it would be over,
Hearth and Home by Christmas Time,
Never knowing what awaited
Upon the firing line.
The intensity of battle, the destruction of human kind,
Disintegration of the life, they had loyally left behind
And hoped one day, to resume, was changed when they did come,
The peaceful days of Edwardian England had ceased upon the Somme.

The Beauty of Rain

Oh how I love the rain!
The rain patters on the windowpane.
I think to myself, am I insane,
Loving, as I do, the pitter patter of the rain?

Falling, falling, like drops of crystal
Dancing upon the pavements
Once grey and murky, now glowing and clean.

Rubbish that once littered the gutters
Now flows away, lost from sight, by speed
Swirling along in the rain's endless power.

How sweet and clear, and clean.
The rain unvarnishes the hidden secrets of the world,
Praise be, if only for the rain!

The rain is ceasing, like the pitter-patter of children's feet,
Softly, slowly, never stopping
Then comes the silence, the peace.

The rain has gone, leaving a breath of freshness,
A world now cleaned by God's own hand,
Daring to show, its beauty, its grace.

Oh how I love, the rain.

Jane Dyson

Symbol of Slaughtered Youth

The early days of September, Summer's on the wane,
Along the abundant hedgerows, Spring seems to have come again.
Amongst the withered leaves and shrubs the Poppy can be seen,
Raising its blood red head to catch every autumn gleam.
The Poppy is the symbol, of when in days of yore,
The Empire's youth was slaughtered on the inhospitable Gallipoli shore.

Its blood red petals represent the blood that was spilled to save us all.

When war was finally over, and we honoured the noble dead,
The blood red Poppy was the symbol, causing many grief and shame,
Shame for having slaughtered those whose innocent youth
Was vanquished in consuming hate, for what was gained, forsooth?
Nought that really mattered, as was proven when once again
Man faced a foe beyond the realms of our country's domain.

Its blood red petals represent the blood that was spilled to save us all.

THE POETRY LIBRARY

Let Love Blossom in Your Heart for All

Today is such a dismal day
For those with lonely hearts,
While those around are revelling,
In gifts from their sweethearts.

The budding rose,
The chocolates,
The cards unsigned but known,
The endearing voice, speaking on the telephone.

Let us not forget them,
Though romance is breaking free,
As we revel in our cherished dreams
Of happy families.

Everyone is not so lucky,
That their dreams can come true.
Perhaps that lonely heart,
Belongs to me or to you.
Let love blossom in your heart for all.

Remembrance of Emily

Though long has set the sun that bathed your youthful brow,
Enchanting imagination, still unforgotten now,
Though age of more than a century,
Has parted your soul from Earth's insecurity.

The imagination that once wove from dreams,
Characters long enduring, so they seem.
With machinations of the most unchristian view,
Even modern day, produces a few.

Who have not learnt the lessons of your age
Continue to believe that life's a stage
Upon which they may strut and offend
Those whose images of life they can never comprehend.

Yet Gondal imagery can still inspire the few
Who listen to your words, and substance too.
Transforming those everyday occurrences
Into magical kingdoms where they alone can dwell.

Unencumbered by their daily toil, the sorrows, the strife,
Riven from the beauties of life,
You passed this way but once, and then were gone,
But your memory and feelings linger on and on.

In those of us who trust to life's unending reign
In heaven, free from anguish and pain,
Where both your sisters shortly follow thee,
Where father finally arrived to complete the family tree,
Riven as it was, from obscurity.

Denied as you were, your portion of human fame,
Unfettered by life or social chain,
Your spirit dwells within the Yorkshire Dales,
Treasured for eternity, Emily.

Jane Dyson

The Challenge of Peace

The drums beat, the thunder rolls, but to all they call in vain,
The carnage on our streets makes eyes turn inwards with shame.
What is it, that causes others to take life,
To feud with their neighbours, to revel in religious strife?

Can nobody out there realise the cause
That manifests itself, in battle-hungry jaws?
What no one seems to notice, and no one understands,
For peace to come to Ireland, to silence the terrorist bands

Needs all to pull together, not separated by their creeds!
Extend your hand in friendship, and multiple good deeds.
Only then have we the chance of reaching an understanding,
And patching up the rift of such long standing.

Band together all, let peace and peace alone be your aim!
This bloody reign of terror is playing the devil's game.
Put aside your differences, bury family feuds,
Relinquish animosity—let Jesus preach the truth.

Be friends, be friends together, no matter what your creed,
Its time to come together and heal the breach between us,
To cast aside our doubts, to trust to others' fears,
And let the dust of conflict be buried deep in cheers.

Plea From the Heart

Hidden from view, it might be,
But it's there all the same, in you and me.
But others jeer and make life a curse
Because a gene has stamped us apart!
Apart from the rest, who do not understand
That it's no fault of ours, I think you'll agree,
God made us what we happen to be.

It wasn't by choice we feel as we do,
Favouring our own sex, as we do,
But why should we hide what isn't our fault?
Just because society is riven with doubt
They treat us as queer, unnatural things,
Though they to us are unnatural too,
Yet we do not snigger and jeer at what they choose to do.

So why can't they just leave us alone?
Because of their attitude we hide and fear,
Huddled in closets, filled with doubt.
Some of our brethren are homophobic and cruel,
Chastisement seems to be but the rule.
Deal with us kindly, let us relate,
Even now, it's never to late.

We are one species, so why disagree?
Meet us as brothers and sisters, in harmony.

Jane Dyson

We might not fit in, but give us the choice.
This hidden gene should be no disgrace.
God deemed what we were meant to be.
We look no different from you, you'll agree,
So why send us to purgatory?

Hidden by Time

Marching forward, ever on,
The pounding feet,
The beat of the drum.
Khaki figures stand in line,
Interspersed with blue and red, the colour of wine.

The bugles call, the men respond,
Denied their comforts,
England must stand strong!
Youthful innocents stand and fight,
Torn from their loved ones, earthly delight.

Forward, ever onwards, into the void,
War leaves nothing untouched.
No innocence survives,
Bent on destruction, for their evil ends,
Parts families, loved ones and faithful friends.

Though years do pass,
Wounds of the body do heal,
But the styles of humanity remain for all, yet a few,
Those whose lives are too short to rue,
Their echoing tramp remains for all time.

Names long forgotten, still reveal the pain:
Mons, Somme, Verdun, Ypres.

Jane Dyson

The chilling sounds of battle echo in the trees.
Forward, ever onwards, silent they pass,
Those ghostly marching soldier boys drift past.

The Tearful Years

When we were young we learnt to stand and wait,
While mothers gossiped at the gate.
We hung around, never uttering a sound,
Never daring to interfere,
But always knowing, always aware,
That should we want them, they'll be there.

Who are they that offer so much?
They are our 'parents' in whom we can place all our trust.
Who not many consider,
When in our youth we rave and rebel,
But do they ever really condemn us,
To our just fate?
Think carefully—before it's too late.

The Passage of Time

As time doth pass us by,
I sometimes yearn for what has been.
In another century, now unseen.
When life was more balanced, but not emancipated,
As is our right today.
Though they had less freedom, they did have respect,
For those of an age, older than themselves.
Children remained, seen but unheard,
But at the forefront of all, they followed Christ's teaching.
Pay reverence to that power, merciful and just.
Which in modern times seems regarded as Bible bashing and distrust.
Members of society not only deny
But forget the reliance, in which we might trust,
Every minute, every day, making life's labours more just.

Days of Yore

What has become of the homely skills,
The knitted sweaters to keep out the chills,
Children's summer dresses, and patchwork quilts?
These skills, once taught, have passed beyond our ken,
The thrifty housewife and her creative yen.
No longer do mothers sit and knit,
or darn their children's rents and tears!
No one bothers, no one dares.
It's so much easier to trot down to town and buy them new.

Factory made, with no loving touch,
The touch that to some meant so much.
Like the boys in the trenches,
Receiving packets from home,
With knitted socks and knitted vests,
Blessed with mother's love,
To swathe that boyish breast,
Beneath which, beats a heart so true.

Where have they gone, these homely cares,
Eaten up in the vortex, as time moves on?
No one has time anymore
To teach the skills women learned in days of yore,
Girls enter motherhood, knowing nothing more
Than that everything baby needs is at the superstore.
Motherhood has lost its grace,
Succeeded by the never-ending rat race.

Time is Running Out

Remove the cars, vans and lorries,
Once seen as the pinnacle of endeavour;
Now their presence is stealing our very lives,
Adding pollution and destroying our atmosphere.

Regenerate the human machine, place it back where it belongs,
God made it as a useful tool, not something deemed a fool
To cause death and destruction;
Release it from its bondage, give it a new resolve!

Without cars, vans and lorries, death rates would fast diminish,
Pollution would reduce, giving the needy ozone a chance to replenish;
If not, before many days are past, the world will be no more.
Neither man, machine or animal will remain, the planet desolate
For ever more.

What use, then, will such luxuries be,
With no living soul to witness, to see.
Remove the source before it's too late,
We may then gain the chance to see and wait.

If not, our doom is looming ever nearer!
Time is running out, danger stands before us.
Do not hesitate at the last, but give in now:
If we all pull together, we will save ourselves, somehow.
Act now, now, now!

Journey of theMind

Time hath come, to take a journey all will someday fulfil,
When one bends their steps to heaven's gate.
But pause, before it's too late.
Reassess, how modern life has slighted
The honour and the glory due
To He, to whom we must all meet on the day of reckoning.

Turn back time to the days of ancestral worship,
Let one's eyes roam over elegant architecture,
The beauties of historic stained glass,
Follow in your ancestor's footsteps.
Tread forward, firmly, resolutely, with ones heart open to the Lord.
Think not of the cost, the time wasted, honouring the unseen.

Instead, revel in the stateliness of architecture, long forgotten,
As in the beauties seen from the transept,
As you mentally stride, resplendent in your unseen armour,
To lift up your sword in the cause—
A cause which is just, and which in modern times
Has vanished from the traditional Sunday role of numerous Britons.

Aberdaron

To Aber we came, we soldiers in Christ,
Prepared for all hazards,
To keep our tryst.
We followed the paths of those gone before,
From England to Gwyneddian shore.
St Winifred, St Bueno, and many more,
Were asked, and did grant, the strength to proceed.

We arrived at the gateway,
For crossing the Sound,
No one but angels could cross in one bound.
Boiling seas, torrential rain, whistling winds arose,
Nature has closed the way ahead.
Worn, weary but undaunted, we retired to bed.
Next day we arose, and viewed from the headland
The goal of the pilgrimage: Bardsey Island.

Forgotten Meaning

Midnight tolls, the bells proclaim,
But do they chime their message, in vain
Telling of the Lord's lowly birth,
In a stable, here on earth?
Men no longer hearken, men no longer hear,
Being filled with an abundance
Of merriment and Christmas cheer.

For all who are alone,
For all, whose hearts are sad,
The tolling of the bells reminds one
Of what man once had.
Forgotten is the message, unheeded the heavenly call,
Who calls, but no one hears now,
Forgotten by one and all.

Christmas is no longer a time of thought and prayer,
People no longer care, for the sacrifice He made.
Dying on the cross,
Absolving man from sin,
Man heedeth not, man careth not,
What once was held supreme.

Mercantilist passions
Have taken that sanctified place,
More thoughts expended on baubles,

Than on the human race.
The bells might toll forever,
Their message, forgotten in the dim and distant past,
While God hides his eyes in sorrow,
Will turn from man alas.

Faded Memories

"Merry Christmas!" Children call, as they tumble out of bed,
Poignant memories are most dear,
But what remains, in their stead.
The merry days of childhood,
Other pressing matters,
Wipe the memory pictures,
From the brain's small store.

What grief, this getting older is, to those like me,
Who would wish to be returned,
To that time, beneath the Christmas tree.
Too much juggling of finances,
Wrapping up those dainty gifts,
That once the day is over,
Will be forgotten ever more,
Or join the toys of yesteryear, or from the year before.

But oh! To return to childhood,
If only for Christmas day,
And lead the life unheeding,
In each and every way.
We then might thus endure,
Adult stagnation for 364 more days,
To have the chance of reliving,
Those magical halcyon days

Jane Dyson

When one was but a child,
Delving into the Christmas sock
To learn what gifts and prizes had fallen to our lot:
Prizes given for being good,
Or rewards for trying hard,
To refresh those fading memories
Of times which were so good
But will never come again.

Spare a Thought

Spare a thought,
For those who care,
For those of us who could despair,
Huddled in boxes, or on the streets,
Far from those who love and care,
Spare a thought for those who need
Our thoughts and prayers.

Peace

In these days, lets stop and think,
Isn't it time to extend a hand, in Peace?
Now Peace is spreading across the world:
Be thee rich or poor,
Reach out and touch
Those around
Who may be less well off
Than you and me.
Learn well the line,
In the Lord's Prayer,
"Forgive those, who trespass against us,"
For this will ensure,
That Peace rules the day,
Rather than War, Revenge and Terrorism,
Let us leave our revenge to God,
The Merciful.

Hive of Industry

Now welcome the coming of the new day
That changes life to some degree,
The myriad of the busy, bustling commuters.
Hustling to their daily toil,
Intent only on reaching their destination,
No thought for any but themselves,
The relentless clock that binds them,
Through every working day,
Toils on and on.
Until the clock allows them
To cease work, and
Turn their thoughts to play.
What would these beings be
Without the clock's insistent drive
Governing their lives so fully?
They are lost, yet no one is to blame
But them, themselves, for this.
This is the choice they have chosen,
The choice, gives freedom of a kind,
But the clock tolls on and on.

Hidden World

Wandering through the city streets people no longer stand and stare
At the hidden shanty dwellers of whom most are not aware.
Who are these shanty dwellers, these sufferers of fate
Who exist, hidden from the seeing eyes and the caring bounties of the state?

They dwell in cardboard boxes, their clothes ragged and unclean;
No access have they to the sanitation we take as our just mean.
These shanty dwellers dwell among the rubbish and garbage, unseen,
Some knowing little of the pleasant side of life.

Others, consciously declining, to live in accepted ways,
Glorifying in their freedom, but suffering from winter's many malaise,
They do not fear the weather, the cold, the snow or the rain,
But wander scavenging for what they need, or incommoding shoppers
with their sad refrains.

"Can you spare twenty pence for tea?" they ask as one passes by.
Many shed the requested pittance, never knowing for what it's really sought,
But to console their conscience, con amore,
For when the day is over, in fine fettle they will be.

With enough purloined silver to make the night pass happily,
Aided with strong liquor, or possibly a shot to remove the reality of their lot,
A little whitish powder they dream dreams of fantastic sort,
These shanty dwellers with whom we sometimes must consort.

Pandora's Box

Open only, if you dare,
And if you do, show courage and prayer,
For in that box, contained therein,
Be all of man's mortal sin
Which God alone has garnered in.

The sin that was released on mortal man
When Adam and Eve faltered from the master's plan.
And so they altered man's destiny,
By folly portrayed, beside a tree.
Wherein there lurked the key to man's desire,
To the consternation of his mighty sire,
And thus brought upon himself the justly ire
Which punished he for his transgression,
But still availed him of his compassion,
For the flaws he showed, are in us all.
Those raised on high must surely fall.
So God deemed for his children one and all,
To build too high they must tumble and fall,
To learn the truth of their transgression,
To overcome their obstacle of fate,
To learn to heed him, before it's too late.
To bow their heads, and follow his rules,
Disregarded now only by heedless fools.
Follow God's unhindered path,
Commit not the folly of days long past,

Jane Dyson

Do not open that box of sin,
Or you yourself will be drawn within.
Pandora's box is full of sin:
Hold tight to prayer, don't wander in!

Countdown to Chance

Saturday night, the clock strikes eight,
Sitting rigid in the chair with fingers crossed,
Eyes tight shut.
As the balls go a tumbling, round and around,
Then the countdown has started, there isn't a sound.
The button is pressed, our prayers climb to God,
And soon now, we could be, in seventh heaven.
One by one, the numbers fall,
White and yellow, pink and green, then blue,
Matching our mood as we surely know
Our luck has failed us, again and again!
But we still are given reason to pause:
Can it be real, you wonder again,
Your chance has come, and gone while you weren't aware!
That's what happens when Lottery fever's in the air.

To Angel, My Friend

Oh angel dearest, I can see nothing but woe, in what you propose to do,
I do not know,
God made you as you are, so why seek to change, a personna, like a
dying star, is not easy to arrange.
Removal of bodily parts can surely make no difference,
It's what's within your heart and mind that's pure and still unsullied.
The skin is but an envelope, wrapped around us to protect those feelings,
Buried deep inside every person's breast.

They make us what we are, unique and yet the same,
Like following the guiding star to fame or shame.
Destroy the outer wrapping, but remember, those who care
Will not witness the physical change without feelings of despair.
Life as was will no longer be, for you are not the same: be careful,
Go cautiously.

Before you're touched by the knife, even wielded scientifically,
It seems wrong to tamper with one's life, and so unnecessary.
Rethink your intentions, be brave and face the truth,
Do not deny your imperfection, but seek solitude, reflection and truth.
Remember, you can never be what once you were before:
Take care, my angel dearest, my *con amour*.

Ladies of the Night

Innocent as a new-born babe, held tenderly in mother's arms,
Never dreaming what this life will be, unable yet to understand her charms.
Round every corner there doth lurk, societies degrading trade,
Men waiting, but to touch and abuse,
Defaming and despoiling goods
What God created oh so pure, forever wanting more and more.
She smiles, just like an innocent, but pain now covers sin:
From the hands of God she's fallen and taken up her stand,
Offering lithesome, supple tempting treats, for sale to those who'll dare,
Extolling life's erotic realms, never flinching, never a care,
So long as they can meet the cost,
What matter, the angel's lost.
Her innocence and modesty, she seeks no judgement from her life,
All she craves she has and more, but searches ever on,
For but one thing she desires, her trade does not provide.
Financial bounty she can but gain, but security is denied.
Drifting on from place to place, never having roots
But the crisp crackling sound of commercial gain
And the tramping of many boots.
Poor child, she's truly lost her way, having become a slave of man
And yet
Is she truly shamming, this angel of the night?

Jane Dyson

Judgement's Clock

The Cathedral clock chimes the hour
The congregation saunters on
Beside the roadways and the walls
Human flotsam and jetsam linger on.

Their eyes seem to ask of any who pause:
"Stay your steps stranger, give us a break!"
Life is too full, nobody cares
The seconds are ticking, hearken who dares.

Take up this chance of showing compassion.
The Father of all would hinder you not
But enter one's name in the listings of Lot
Whose own wife did not hearken, but turned into salt.

Such bitterness canst be avoided, so never doubt
The chimes striking are for your ears alone:
Mankind may but falter, but never alone,
Walking unblended, comes to the throne.

Honour is bestowed where honour is known:
Treat us with kindness, whatever you do.
Attain your adjudgment at the day's weary end:
Surrender your piety, my faithful friend.

The Future Foretold

Though we do try to cut down the waste,
It never seems to lessen at the garden gate.
We recycle paper, glass and cardboard,
But civilisation wants to do nothing but hoard.
Hidden in attics and numerous places
The harder one searches, the more is revealed
And not knowing how it's been concealed.

In days long gone, they wrapped goods in paper,
Now they all cry, "Save our trees,"
but they do not change to suit every need.
They stop the paradise, so they say conserve,
But generate more problems by the score
Producing plastic and cardboard and styrene containers
Saying they are biodegradable.
But why not just paper, as days long gone by,
recycling what's left stifling the cry?

Instead they create ever increasing mountains of refuge
Which will remain when we're long gone,
Leaving evidence for historians, in the dim and distant future,
If any future remains, creating images of the civilisation which has gone.
It will outlive us, no matter how long we linger on.
So save your breath, and change to one's need,
Replacing the plastics and styrene with paper indeed.

Man's Destiny Foretold

Toiling through the years we go,
To what end, we do not know,
Aspiring, grasping, ever wanting,
Killing, thieving, never listening,
Forgotten in ages past.
Sounds muted, we move that fast.
That poor, unheeded Christianity
Pleads with us to stop and consider
But we don't hear our own souls register.
The word that is, man's only salvation,
Not the constant clicking, of computerisation.
Our souls are barren, we don't heed,
Our spiritual sanctity, whatever one's creed.
The day will come, when Judgement falls,
Echoing round barren walls
That should have nurtured God's grace,
Instead of following greed's endless chase.
Heed the call, now, before the end,
Take God as your ever loving, faithful friend.

Broken Union

You clung to life in my despite, and carved your place anew,
Banishing me from everything,
purity and gentleness you used all through,
Though you were just a year old babe, you filled me with despair,
Wounded, crying, forbidden death, I turned away at last.
Broken both in body and heart, my days filled with woe,
To live my life in emptiness, in desolation you will never know.
I flitted from one experience to another, but nothing brought me rest,
The years tolled by, you never knew who I was or why,
As each day passed, you grew, and I was left, barren and dry.
You grew into someone strange and kind,
But someone I'd never know,
You locked me out of your life, made me seek for something new.
Time it was that healed the pain, but still it left its mark.
Is motherhood for all, the same, or does this affect just me and you?
Life my dear will never be the same since parting from you,
But for the best it must have been.
You suffered little by the change, Your heart is whole, at rest,
That's because my precious babe, You're You!

Jane Dyson

In Memorial

There she stands, so white, so still,
Always in her place,
Watching with those loving eyes,
Clasped hands before her face.

She marks the spot where my heart lies,
Buried beneath the soil.
Guarding and protecting thine,
Until once more, we're side by side

And meet, and never more shall part
In God's compassionate Grace.
But where's my little Angel gone?
There's no longer any trace.

She stood where I had placed her:
For years she's marked your grave.
But now she's been removed.
Who's stolen my little Angel dear
Without whom I cannot move.

She must be found, she must be traced,
To mark your grave anew.

* * *

THE POETRY LIBRARY

I've found my missing Angel,
Fallen flat upon her face.

To right her would be just,
But can I take that chance
To immortalise your resting place,
though you be turned to dust?

Her lips are kissing you, my love,
You, I love so very much.

The Clock of History

Tick, Tock, the grand clock
Never sleeping, never ceasing,
Counting out the minutes, of every century.
Recording all that happens, sequentially.

Races change and falter
Never comprehend
How history's the greatest teacher,
Man's mind could comprehend.

In 1899, we fought the Zulu wars.
For what did man do this?
For conquering foreign shores,
Slaying innocent natives, for what he did not own.

Committing crimes unthinking
For which history shall atone.
Always seeking something, better than the rest,
Never contented, to set aside, and rest.

Forging always on, for some unattainable goal,
Restless, ever seeking, demanding control.
But what does he gain, from his vain inglorious fight,
History can but tell us when the TIME is right.

What are Friends?

What are friends?
I do not know
Maybe mythical figures
From long ago.

Friends we all need
But how do we tell,
If they are real
Or imagined just so…

Just so that we
Can feel they exist,
My friends and I
Do not dwell in houses

We roam the fields
Hedgerows and skies
Some of them live
In the seas by and by.

Who are these friends?
To whom I am speaking
They are not human
I think you'll agree

They are but part
Of God's great creativity,
No axe to grind
No condemnation.

They it is
Who are loyal and true
Who give you their love
Every day, through and through.

Consider This?

The bare branches
So long, blowing in the breeze.
Now blossom into freshness
In the Spring.
Buds bursting open,
Leaves uncurl and wave,
Making each day, beautiful and sweet,
Oh what a pleasure, what a treat.
Never thinking,
That one day,
Through our own carelessness,
All will vanish, leaving
The Earth, bare and bleak.

How do We Know?

White is the page of the paper we write
So clean, so pure, such a delight.
Like the child that we nurture, so sweet and so pure,
Contamination comes only with life.
The habits, the fears, the despair, the delights
Do the taints then appear, destroying the purity and light.

Goodness and light, turning the purity
Into the darkness of Hell, we endure,
Caused not by nature, so sweet and so pure.
Blighted by civilization, its greed to ensure,
Conform we must, and thus we endure the night
For this flight is endless, a devil's delight.

Have we the strength, we alone,
To fight for the light, and so atone,
Turning away from the greed of our peers
Striving for beauty, through endless years.
Have we the strength, the will to succeed,
How do we know, unless we do try,
Alone or together, you and I.

Wash Day Praise

Lines full of washing
Flapping in the breeze
Colours of many hues
Enlivening the drab backyards
Filling everywhere with colour
The freshly laundered linen
Mingles with the natural scents
Of natures garlands of beauty
Heaven scent.
Oh these wondrous washing days of Spring.

Jane Dyson

Enter the Light

What took me so long
To see the light
Now it shines
Both day and night.

When that brown envelope
Drops through the door
Wondering just what
Will be in store.

Rejection has lost
It's piercing sting,
Now I know, the pleasure
Success can bring.

Fame and fortune
Are far away
But I shall not
Rue the day.

When Lantern Light
Arrived at last
Depression now
A thing of the past.

How I wish
I'd known years before
So now I'd like
To even the score.

Now is not the time
To hide your light
Under a bushel
Burning bright.

Life on the Edge

Living on the edge, that's what we do
Always the one at the end of the queue,
Filling out forms, papers galore
The answers the same, which we abhor.
Rejected, rejected, but what can we do?
We are the numerous, jobs are so few.
They cry out for workers, but we get no chance
The positions the same, we never advance.
So in this rut we must just sit,
Who can we turn to, who gives a shit.

Life without hope, misery and pain,
We who must sit here, aint it a shame!
Work without pay, we can have without doubt
But how can this help us out?
It won't pay the bills, the rent or the tax,
We might just as well sit back and relax.
Life without work, that is our doom,
Give us the chance to show what a boon
We can but add to the society in which we dwell;
Give us some pride, not this insufferable hell!

The World of Childhood

Boldly he goes Small of stature
Sturdy as a tree
A child with purpose
Unknown to you and me.
What is he thinking
What does he see,
Is his life heaven, or hell,
Unknown to the likes of you and me.

What is He feeling
So young, yet so bold,
Faced with a world, full of mysteries untold.
Of what He will find,
Around every corner,
What lurks behind.
Yet boldly He goes
Exploring at will,
What will he find,

Something to fear, or to thrill.
How do we know,
What this child does see,
Is it a dinosaur?
Is it a tree?
Childhood is a world
None understand

Except for those
Who view it, at close hand.

The land of the child
Is his special place
Adults are unwelcome
Even a disgrace.
What is this land,
So foreign, and strange,
Once we all knew it
But has it all changed,
This world of childhood?

The Silent Guardian

Who is that calling through the trees?
Soft wings beat, planing the breeze.
Stealthily moving through the quiet of the night,
Giving rodents the fright of their life.

Occasionally you hear it call to its brethren,
Twit Twoo, Twit Twoo,
Roosting in woodlands, hardly seen,
Who is this mysterious visitor, across the green?

Once they were well known, now they are few,
Rarities they've become, apart from the zoo.
So lordly they look, when one happens to see,
The mysterious barn owl, flying free.

The woodlands dwindle, but this did not stop
The barn owl from nesting on our outcrop,
In farms and churches, towers and trees;
These are the places where they did breed.

Gone are they, all but a few
Killed by technology, and humans too,
All that is, apart from the few,
Who still treasure the odd one or two.

But we'd better watch out, for he is so few,
If we don't take care, then what will we do?
The rats would take over, then so would the Plague,
Without the silent guardian, almost extinct.
My friend and yours, the barn owl is he
We must protect him, both you and me.

Down the Vole Sacree

Down the road they came at last,
Many who, would breathe their last,
Staunch defenders, one and all,
Outnumbered by the Hun.
They obeyed their country's need,
But those though doomed,
Do bravely bow,
Holding together, Lord knows how,
Amidst the slaughter, there unfurled,
A credit to the race of men,
Who do not shirk the onerous call,
Man and boy, they need them all,
Where? You ask, is this the case
At Verdun, where they stand and face,
Denying evil, access,
Keeping closed the door, and mitigating distress,
For should Verdun totter and fall,
It would be the end, for one and all.
But bravely they stand, alone and fight,
Against the Kaiser's maw and might,
In bygone days they now shall be,
Ever remembered in His…story.
Though Verdun may falter,
We do not blame,
Those brave young souls,
Ensnared in war's fell game.

We salute thee, one and all,
God bless thee lads, you heeded the call.

The Loss of Society

Whatever's become of society,
When once people stood,
Gossiping over walls and fences,
Leaning on brooms,
Enquiring of others "What News?"

If one did not show, someone came to find out,
What was the matter, and if they could help?
All is now gone, where,
Concern used to tread,
Everyone's filled with feelings of dread.

People have no time now,
As they used to do,
Hours of the day are crowded all through,
The pace of life, has changed for the worse,
Business has become, the modern day curse.

One's neighbours unknown, pass by in the street,
Eyes that once met, now scarcely meet.
Everyone shuns, those all around,
Fearing the reaction, should they step out of line,
The community feeling has withered with time.

Everyone's now, a social outcast,
The once, English Gentry, a thing of the past,

Gone from our culture, never to return,
Unless we force ourselves, to show others concern,
Concern is now scorned, as a weakness within,

Driven out from our hearts, by continuous sin.
Isn't it time we back pedalled a bit,
Recapturing the community spirit.
Retracing the rules, our ancestors held,
Recovering our pride in our nation all through.

Ringing the Changes

Big Ben doth chime throughout the night
When citizens should be sleeping,
But many stand and wait, until he ceased tolling.
He proclaims the birth of a New Year, but will the new,
Be different from what went before?
Will the slaughter, terror, crime, brutality and degradation
Stop as does his chime, affecting every nation.
Or will it continue to blight our lives,
Filling newspapers, radio's and television.
Depressing our very lives,
One would think, when one was born,
That we enter first into Hell, and only after death is past,
Can we taste that heavenly spell.
For gone are all restraints,
Which tames society to some degree,
Anarchy and despotism are the norm, for all to see.
Why can we not content ourselves, and build only for the better,
Instead of wrecking others' things, and placing them in fetters,
Gone is the calm and balmy past, never more to return,
We cannot turn back the clock and gain from what has gone.
But must we so depreciate the wonders God provides
By lusting after others' gain, never content, always divided?

II

Stories and Prose

School's Out

"Sarah Robbins, Did you hear what I just asked? Then answer the question please." Miss Philpots' voice sounded shrill and angry. The other pupils turned to stare at Sarah. Sarah was oblivious to what was going on around her. It was only when Miss Philpots banged on her desk that Sarah became aware that she was actually in school, not lost in a dream world of her own choosing.

"Well, Sarah." The teacher's fingers were tapping—a sure sign she was getting really angry. Then, to make matters worse, Sarah asked, "Excuse me, Miss Philpots—could you please repeat your question?"

"Really Sarah, you're behaving like a little first former, not like the young lady you are, and a fifth former at that. Go and stand outside the room! I'll talk to you later! We've wasted enough time this morning as it is. The exams are nearly upon us and some people here want to pass those exams. Now leave the room." The last words were spoken with her anger barely suppressed. Smiling self-consciously at her classmates, Sarah drifted out of the room.

Once outside the door she quickly glanced at her watch. Plenty of time yet before the end of the lesson. She would just stand here and dream of what life would be like after school had finished. She hated school. Everyone telling her to do this, do that, and never allowing her to do what she dreamed of. Well, they'd see.

Lost in a world of her own, Sarah was soon imagining what she'd do when school was out. She had high hopes. There was a certain young man she'd had her eye on now, for months, but he never seemed to notice her.

She knew he was a student. She saw him every afternoon in the coffee bar where she and her friends gathered to discuss the local talent. He seemed extremely tall to her dainty five-foot nothing, and his hair was the colour of jet, and it literally glistened when the sun shone on it. Those smoky grey eyes seemed to gaze straight through her, yet she tingled whenever she thought he was looking her way. The only thing she didn't know was his name.

In her imagination he was her prince charming, and she his princess just like in the fairy tale, but he was real—a real man who had captured her heart.

As in the fairy tale, when the clock struck midnight, the ringing of the bell for break brought her back to earth with a bump. Her classmates were streaming past her. One of her friends would occasionally raise an eyebrow as she passed, knowing that for once Sarah was really in trouble; but none dared to wait and see what the outcome would be. Miss Philpots was well known in the school for her wicked temper.

As the last classmate passed her, she heard the teacher's voice. The intervening time had done nothing to calm her down. "Sarah Robbins, come here please."

With blue eyes staring defiantly ahead, Sarah walked back into the room, her golden mane swirling round her shoulders. She knew she was in trouble, but for once she couldn't give a damn. Her prince charming was always there, locked in her memory, to soften the sting of the teacher's words.

"Now Sarah, it was not like you. You're not usually so inattentive in my class. Please explain your behaviour if you can." The scorn in the teacher's voice was clear. She had taught Sarah and her classmates since they started at the school. Sarah had always been one of her brighter pupils, and she was at a loss for a reason why, this close to the end of her school life, she should suddenly decide to play the fool.

"Well, Sarah—lost for words?" Miss Philpots tapped her desk. In an almost inaudible voice, Sarah spoke. "I'm sorry Miss Philpots. What did you say?"

Miss Philpots stared. Was the girl crazy or couldn't she hear properly? Determined to test the theory, Miss Philpots turned and wrote something on the board behind her. Sarah watched, comprehension dawning.

Then, as the teacher finished writing, Sarah wrote beneath her words: I apologise sincerely Miss Philpots but the lessons sound like double Dutch. Most of what you say sounds just like a rumbling to me. Maybe there is something wrong with my hearing. I don't mean to act the fool or annoy you. Sarah.

Having read and understood Sarah's predicament, Miss Philpots picked up her pen and notebook and quickly wrote a short letter. Then, folding the paper over, she wrote another message on the board. It read, Take this to the Headmaster. He will tell you what to do. Do you understand?

As the teacher turned back to her, Sarah nodded and held out her hand. Miss Philpots gave her the note and watched as she left the room. Miss Philpots was puzzled. Hadn't the girl's parents noticed anything, but then, thinking it over, she saw the possible reason why.

Sarah was the second oldest—one of five children. With four others around maybe her mother simply hadn't noticed the child's suffering. Sarah was such a quiet little thing, tending to withdraw from company as a whole, apart from her two chums she had made early on in life and stuck to throughout school. She hoped this would not seriously affect the child's future. Sarah was such an intelligent child. It would be a shame if, because of this problem, she threw everything away and married some totally unsuitable young man.

Miss Philpots could almost visualise it. He would be tall and good-looking, but like her mother before her, he would lumber her with a huge family and hardly any money. A sheer waste of natural talent, that's what it would be. The child, still innocent of the fickle ways of men, would believe someone was her prince charming come to rescue her from oblivion.

Stranger than Fiction

Winter held the country in its freezing grip. There was little chance for any sport, but it was a good time for listening to stories beside a crackling log fire! At one such evening, with many a jar to jolly the teller along, Winston Tasker sat, enjoying what, he declared, was a well deserved pint. Then the story-telling began.

That night it was the turn of a couple of old timer's who rehashed a story from their youth—when both themselves and their mates were in one or other of the services doing their national service. Sid it was who told the tale, and it was enough to chill the strongest amongst the audience. Winston was no exception. Sid began…

"It was the winter of 1950. We'd just gone back in to camp after strolling back through the village wanting to know about a sight we'd seen. The locals had assured us that the graves, for that was what we were curious about, belonged to a horse and two dogs. These creatures were reputed to have belonged to Lady Ramsbottom.

It was said that back in the last century her husband had slaughtered the animals in a fit of pique. She never forgave him. She vowed that he would rue the day he killed her devoted pets. He thought nothing of this for he was a blasé fellow who, like the disciple Thomas, doubted that anything would make him repent of his actions. Time was to prove just how wrong he was.

A month to the day that the dreadful deed had occurred, Lady Ramsbottom took her own life. She had selected the date to pay back her husband. The horse and dogs had been buried with magnificent marble headstones set where they lay, their names emblazoned in gold leaf.

Her husband returned from a hunting expedition to find her body, dressed in white, lying on their matrimonial bed. Her ebony hair framed her peaceful face, but her eyes stared at him, making him shudder. Not knowing what was in store for him, he retired before his fire for his evening meal. He had one more chore to perform before he retired for the night.

Lighting his lantern, he strolled around the grounds, passing close to the woods that were part of the estate. There he froze. Riding through the woods on a horse was a lady, the image of his dead wife—her white gown a perfect foil for her ebony hair. Her eyes seemed to gleam with hate for him out of the darkness.

When the vision, if vision it was, had passed, he fled, vowing never to return." Sid's voice died as he drew his recital to its close, as his audience thought, but he still had something to add.

"That, friends, was what we had been told in the village; but neither my mate or myself believed it until, the very next night, we heard the same tale—but some fifty years later than the villagers had foretold. A mate of ours, one Jimmy Blatt who was an M.P in the R.A.F. , never finished his service for patrolling the base. He witnessed the same sight as that which had been witnessed by Lord Ramsbottom on what had become known as 'The Ride of the White Lady.' The day in question was February 28th.

Jimmy himself never recovered from his sighting and was, for the rest of his life, resident in a closed community. His nerves were too stretched by what he had seen to ever mingle with his fellows again."

Sid's voice died away, but no one in the pub moved, whether by the spell cast by Sid's tale or by some other reason. Then, as the Landlord, the only one not frozen in his place, balled out, "Time please," voices began to murmur again.

One by one the audience began to move, some pushing their glasses on to the bar. Many thumped Sid on the back—Winston amongst them, but he felt he had to know. Was this just a tall tale thought up to suit the night, or was it something more?

Going over to Sid, he thumped him on the back, then added: "Well Sid, I've never heard a better tale. It was a tale, wasn't it? Just something to keep the gang amused tonight?" He waited...

Having finished his pint, Sid rose, pulling on his jacket before tucking his scarf round his neck. Then he spoke. "Nay lad, that was no tall tale! That was true, that was. It happened just as I said. Poor Jimmy is to be buried this week. He died never having forgotten the White Lady, and he was seventy only last week."

Winston shivered. Then, leaving the pub with the rest, he began to think about the tale he had heard. He thought it was something that had been written as a penny dreadful from the old boy's past, resurrected to chill his friends at the local. Now, with Sid's disclaimer ringing in his ears, he had to grant that truth could be stranger than fiction. He would have said the tale had come from the pen of someone like Stephen King, but the very fact that poor Jimmy Blatt had never forgotten it persuaded him to believe what he had heard.

Recalling the Past

In today's high tech world, certain aspects which were regarded as an integral part of growing up seem to have been forgotten, or more likely, blatantly ignored. To see the difference, one can do no better than to read two writers whose work gives opposite views of the nineteenth century's view on society, especially that of the middle class—novels, such as Jane Austen's *Pride and Prejudice*, and Emily Brontë's *Wuthering Heights.*

In the Austen novel we see the respect and moral rectitude that was practised, and how people regarded those older than themselves, not as nuisances, but as models that the younger generation were encouraged to follow. In comparison, in the novel by Emily Brontë we are shown how, due to the laxity and intolerances shown in the upbringing of both Heathcliff and Catherine, their adult lives become fraught with dissention. Duplicates of both Hindley Earnshaw and Heathcliff can easily be found throughout our modern society. Men with the character of Wickliff out of Miss Austen's novel can be seen in the same disagreeable light now as then.

Many of the characters depicted in both these novels were not what we today would term rich, but they had something that society seems to have forgotten. They had the care and respect for people older than themselves – people who had taught them from the cradle—whereas so many of today's youth are addicted to some toxic substance, a craving for which wipes out any teaching they may have received, inhibiting them from obtaining their desire. Their God has become Lucre, not Christ, and they prey on the weak, the elderly and the infirm, using violence, having no concept of honour amongst them for their elders.

The getting and possessing of large amounts of money has superseded the religious and moral teachings of our forefathers, to society's disadvantage.

THE POETRY LIBRARY

Though society has certainly advanced since the times of Miss Brontë and Miss Austen, it does not seem to have improved, but to have degenerated. The rich get richer, and palliate their consciences by donating large sums to charities, but are oblivious of how the lust for lucre has corrupted the society in which they live.

If my own opinion was asked, I would recommend all classes of society, which modern day thinking says does not exist, to read and inwardly digest the writings of both these authors, and observe and copy the ways from the past which are utterly deficient in our present day.

A Tour Through Chester

Whether one is historically inclined or not, you cannot help but feel the history literally seeping into your soul when you tour the city of Chester.

Once upon a time it was a Roman stronghold against the marauding Saxons; then again, against the Gaels of Wales, which lies just across the border. The city is still walled with many historical landmarks to show the tourist its Roman past.

There is the Castle. Though ruined, most of its majesty is still visible as you tour the walls which stretch for two miles around the city, though the city boundaries have been extended since that time. There is also the water tower, but lets begin first by walking the walls.

Entering at the top of Frodsham Street, we begin the tour. The first monument we come to is Eastgate. This was rebuilt in 1769 and was the site of Roman and Medieval gates. There is also the famous clock here that commemorates Queen Victoria's Diamond Jubilee in 1897. Next we come to the Kaleyards. Built in 1275 with Royal permission from Edward I it allowed the monks from the Abbey, now the Cathedral, to tend their kitchen gardens that were outside the walls.

As we walk along we pass the Deanery Field, one of the many sites of the legionary barrack blocks within the Roman Fortress. Further along we come to King Charles Tower. It is said that this is the place from where King Charles watched the defeat of his army at the battle of Rowton Moor in 1645. We then pass the Roman Turf Ramparts. This is a grassy bank sloping down behind the City Walls.

A short stretch further along, which is still standing, is known as the Roman Fortress Wall. It is only walkway height and is best seen from the canal bridge just outside the Northgate. Next is Morgan's Mount, a gun emplacement at the foot of the walls. We have now travelled about one mile.

Now heading back, we come to the Roman Angle Tower. This is the site of the north west corner tower. Next is the Water Tower and Gardens. This is a medieval tower that was built to protect the harbour of those times. It originally projected into the estuary.

We then come to the Watergate. This was rebuilt in 1788. It gave access to the harbour in the Middle Ages. Walking past modern properties today, on one side is County Hall where the educational offices of the city are located. On the other side is the Roodee (Chester Race Course). The Roman Quay can be seen at the edge of the racecourse. It is one of the few Roman Quays surviving in Western Europe.

We have now reached Bridgegate. This overlooks the River Dee. The original gateway guarded the only approach to Chester from Wales. On the Dee itself you can see many forms of bird life, especially Mallard Ducks and Mute Swans. We now come to Wolfgate. This was superseded in 1938 by Newgate. Finally, we come to another Roman Angle Tower. This one is the remains of the south east tower of the Roman Fortress. This completes the tour of the walls, but there is much still to see that echoes the past of this fine city.

There are many fine museums such as the Grosvenor. This houses many collections of artifacts and artworks, specifically of Roman origin. There is also the Toy museum and the Military museum. You can find the story of Chester told in an exhibition at the Heritage Centre situated in the famous Roman Rows. These still house many of our modern shops of today.

After all that exercise, I guess you feel like a rest. Head for Grosvenor Park. This has both beautiful gardens and floral displays, with walkways mingling with ruins of an amphitheatre. Here there is a herb walk, specially suited for the blind or partially sighted visitors who can touch the greenery and walk amongst the mingled fragrances.

However, a word of warning. Should you feel like forty winks in the sun, beware of the local poacher. This is not a person, but a group of crafty grey squirrels who will come right up to your hand to take a fancied snack.

Hold your hand out with some peanuts, and they will sit beside you eating the delicacy, unafraid unless you move suddenly. Take care, though, as their bite is painful and they can nip if displeased with your actions. They are charming to behold, and show that, apart from history through the ages, Chester is also home to plenty of natural history even in today's progressive hasty world.

Dreaming of History

Have you ever sat and dreamed of cities in the past? To view how they have changed, and what things have come to pass? In Chester, the Walled City, let your mind just ramble; standing on the Roman walls, let us take a gander.

To dream, we usually close our eyes, drifting off to sleep, but if you wish to witness it, be prepared just to dream with your mind. Settle back now and I'll begin to sketch you such a picture. No facts will be included as to who the people really were. This we don't know.

Hovering above the walled city named by signs such as Deva... Nothing can be clearly seen as mist rolls in, covering the walled city. Standing patiently upon the walls we're aware of bright gleams that occur spasmodically. These are the sentries, posted but unseen; just occasionally we have glimpses of burnished metal as they catch a passing gleam of sunlight, veiled by the mist.

Staring hard, we can just discern the outline of the walls; but listen close and you may hear the tramping of marching feet, market holders crying their wares. A hush descends upon the place that really is most active, but hidden from our searching eyes; no news can be elicited. Then the mist rolls slowly away, and revealed to our gaze is Chester standing for all to purvey, a sprawling, busy metropolis. Gone like the blink of light are the sounds and whispers of a past, but they're always there if one just dares to see – and hear.

Many signs are still about of which the tourist can proclaim, having visited this historic place and learnt its claim to fame. A march around the walls will show how it's grown and spread from what used to be a fortified place hemmed in by quarried stone.

Watch towers on the walls still turn our eyes to the borders, where lies the mighty foes of old, the Celts and the Gaels, who in their time did harry men, fighting to plunder the riches of old Chester town, but not so any longer.

The aggressors have been overthrown by many many legions who, in the dim and distant past, built the might of which we now in late twentieth-century can but get a taste. Of centurions marching brightly clad, in armour all a shimmer—but remember that all this is just a day-dream to remember.

Unspoken Promise

Standing, staring across the overhang of the bridge whose sides are made of chill grey granite stones, I purvey the purl-grey dawn of morning time. Standing there, I ponder to myself what the life is like in the small town that blooms beside the purling waters of the river that the bridge crosses. Then, chilled by the motionless survey, I turn my steps towards the town —of no name.

Like all towns, I suspect it really is called something, but what I do not know—but to me it will always be the town with no name. Not knowing what I would find, I wandered onwards. I had arrived at what had been given as a meeting place by a person I had never seen, but who was, to my way of thinking, almost my double. We shared the same taste in music, the same birthday, day, month and year, and both loved to wander in unfrequented places, discovering for ourselves the beauties revealed by God and nature's bounty.

Now, as I entered the town, I was expecting nothing out of the ordinary, but with my mind far away, trying to fix my mind on the time we had both agreed to, to meet for the first and possibly only time in our lives, I entered.

My eyes glanced round, the town I had deemed to myself, a town sleeping in the pre-lighted dawn of a Sunday morning. A town that would no doubt be filled with ethereal silence, awaiting the breaking of the Sabbath and the ringing of the church bells, but no. What did I behold as into the main street I ventured?

All around me was, as I had first thought, silent, then…As my eyes, the eyes of a stranger to this town, swept over the rows of shops and other buildings that could be placed in any town in any country, there came the sound of running footsteps, but no one to be seen. Then, red light lit up the early morning, dazzling me where I stood.

All was quiet, except for that evil intrusive light, illuminating all that should remain hidden from the eye of the unknown visitor. With my blurred vision I could not see any sign of movement, but my ears caught the sound of hatred passing unseen from building to building, marring the beauty of the old architecture, and revealing the repaired facades of buildings I had first believed to be beautiful edifices of a different era to my own. The town was awakening. Awakening to just another day, of another year in the struggle for the perpetual independence they had been demanding for years uncounted.

Then, as I stood there, a voice spoke in my ear, "Come, it is not safe here for English people to be seen abroad. Follow me, and I will lead thee to safety." The sound of the voice vanished, but, as I turned to look for the speaker, I could just discern a small form, no bigger than a child, but with eons of wisdom in the face, who was beckoning me to follow.

Leaving the scenes of the town with no name behind me, but never forgotten, I went with my guide. The path I was led upon took us at last back to the bridge over the river. There, my guide vanished. Looking down, I saw from my watch that the time set for our meeting was at hand.

I paced along the bridge, unable to rid my mind of that echo of evil I had become aware of in the centre of the town. Then, at a touch, I turned. I found myself looking in to the identical face of one who could easily have been my guide of a few moments before, but this person was my own height, and with waves of hair tumbling over her shoulders in a golden cascade and eyes as green as the greenest emeralds that might adorn a king's crown.

When she spoke, her voice was like an echo of sweetness, as she introduced herself. "God's Greetings, My name is Lisel. Welcome to Ireland." With a smile that set her face alight, she held out her hand as if she were a courtier. As soon as our fingers touched, the fairyland image of her changed, and we became blood sisters from whom nothing could be hidden, though neither of us spoke.

Without a word, she led me, where I do not know; even now the place remains a mystery to me, but what passed between us can never be recreated in words. We left the bank of the river behind, but it felt as though we covered no actual ground. Then, when she stopped, I found myself in the middle of a gloomy sun-dappled woodland where the birds were carolling in the treetops but no sign of human presence could be seen. Seating herself on a bench carved from tree trunks, she pulled me down beside her. Then, her hand touched my dark short cropped hair, and it was as if she had transferred all her knowledge of what had been happening in Ireland to me by that gentle touch.

We spoke not, but our silence bound us together in the cause. That cause was to defeat the evil that had infested this beautiful land, and had for centuries torn it apart. Our hope was, with the help of others of like mind, to heal the hurts of the land and find some means of bringing the people together in peace again.

> *"Oh Emerald Isle, once so fair and green, why do you shed your*
> *blood, before the feet of your queen?"*

I wasn't aware that she or I had spoken, but those words seemed to bring an affinity between us, so that when we parted, in our hearts we knew, no matter what was between us as people, the cause of Ireland was ours together, to mar or to mend as we could. Human passions we felt between us, though neither had touched or spoken of what we felt, but those feelings were unimportant now the shades had been lifted from our eyes. In our hearts we were as one, as in our love of nature we were joined, but in Ireland we had our challenge. That challenge was something only death could end, but even then, if one remained, the other would too; in the heart of the joined, death would not destroy what we had become—a united bond for a united cause for the good of all in the eyes of the one God to all.

Astra's Promise

Adrienne slouched towards what she had been informed would be her new home for the present. Her dark brown eyes stared resolutely at the ground. She wanted to know nothing yet, about where they would be living. Her small soul fumed. She'd been dragged away from school, her home and her friends. The only explanation had been, "We'll explain later," from her disgruntled parents.

Coming to the door, she wandered inside, paying little attention to what was about her. Then, as she reached the end of the hallway, she stopped, and for the first time, raised her eyes to see where she was.

It was a large airy room, decorated for a child. The walls had pictured wallpaper upon them, but what attracted Adrienne was a large mirror at one end. She would not have noticed it, but this one had a girl about her own age standing inside it, smiling.

Slowly, she walked towards the figure, curious to know who she was, and how she came to be inside the mirror, or at least, that was where she assumed she was. Before she could say anything, the figure spoke. She had a soft lilting voice that wasn't quite English. "Hello! Have you come to live here?"

Startled, Adrienne just nodded, then, thinking she'd better speak, she asked, "Who are you?" The figure grinned, and Adrienne suddenly noticed how alike the figure was to herself. She had little time to take this in, for the figure spoke again. "My name is Astra; do come and play with me. It's been such a long time since I had a friend of my own." The figure beckoned to her.

Not knowing quite how she was to go and play with Astra, she walked forwards until she was touching the mirror. Astra stretched her hand out and they were touching. Feeling herself pulled by Astra, Adrienne stepped forwards, and she was inside the mirror. The room around her had disappeared, but something far more interesting had taken its place.

Looking round, she found she was in a totally different environment. No longer was there a cottage set within an English countryside, but she was in the centre of a room, but a room unlike any she had ever seen before except in the history books at school. It was a Roman room, with Roman people chatting and laughing, relaxing on long marble benches padded with cushions. Adrienne stared around her, stunned at where she found herself, but Astra was tugging at her hand, leading her onwards.

Many years later, Adrienne, now grown up and married, stood staring at the cottage with a sense of deja vue. She knew this place, her memory told her, but from when? Forgotten with the passing years was the time she had spent there as a child. Now she had her own daughter and they were buying the cottage for their new home.

Her daughter was tugging at her hand, asking what she was waiting for. Being but ten, the child did not understand her mother's fascination with the place. Adrienne smiled down into dark brown eyes, the same as hers. "Run along in and explore, Astrid; mummy will follow in a little while."

Astrid ran off quite happily, and when Adrienne went inside, she found her daughter talking to a figure she well remembered. "No Astra, my name is Astrid, but mummy's name is Adrienne. If you're sure, I'll come and play with you now, but how do I reach you?"

Adrienne smiled as she heard this statement. She well remembered what had happened when she had gone to play with Astra. She had witnessed many things that the books in school never mentioned, and ever after, she was praised for her depth of knowledge on the Romans.

Astra, catching sight of a grown up, paused. Astrid had not quite reached her, she was half way between this world and Astra's. Then Adrienne spoke. "Hello Astra, still playing your little game on people after all these years?" Astra stared, then spoke. "How do you know me? Have we met before?"

Adrienne smiled, then answered, "Oh yes, we've met, but it was long ago when I was Astrid's age. Never will I forget the time I came over to play with you. Playing with you changed my whole life when I returned to school."

A smile hovered on Astra's lips. Then, with a sad shake of her head, she spoke. "It's a pity you're far too old now to enter my world, but I'll look after Astrid for you. She'll be safe enough with me so long as the mirror never breaks."

Adrienne nodded, then added, "I know she'll be safe with you. I was, and I'm proof you're a safe friend to have, but I hope your promise will hold. The mirror must be terribly old by now, and might break anytime. Please keep your promise and return Astrid to me."

Then, not waiting for Astra's answer, she turned to her daughter and said, "Go ahead, Astra will keep you safe." With that, she turned and quietly closed the door.

Astra drew Astrid through the mirror, into the land her mother had known as a child. She soon became immersed in the doings of Roman life, forgetting her mother and father and discovering the new house and all its secrets. She was swept along on a rapturous tide of history that, until then, she had only touched briefly in her lessons.

Adrienne continued setting up her new home, little thinking of what might befall her daughter. She had little fear for her safety when, suddenly, there sounded an ominous crack. Something had broken.

Filled with sudden fear, she hurried to the end room where the mirror was. Opening the door, she stared. A huge crack had split the mirror in two. Fear for her daughter filled her whole being. Would Astra manage to keep her promise now the mirror was not complete. She hoped so…

Tears dimmed her brown eyes, but there was nothing to do but wait. She believed Astra would somehow send Astrid back to her, but she did not know when that would be, or if it would now be possible. Was Astrid lost in the time of the Romans?

About the Author

I wandered lonely as a cloud
That floats on high o'er vales and hills
When all at once I saw a crowd,
A host of golden daffodils.

(William Wordsworth 1770-1850)

Like the wanderer in Wordsworth's lines, Jane Dyson was lonely and drifting heedlessly through life until touched by the thirst-quenching waters of Jesus Christ. Since then she has utilised all she sees around her for use in her mill of poetical word pictures—pictures that can, if allowed, speak to all people whatever their beliefs.

Notes

Notes

Notes

Notes

Notes

Notes

Printed in the United Kingdom
by Lightning Source UK Ltd.
101273UKS00003B/433-447